GUID TO THE MERRY MAIDENS STONE CIRCLE

AND OTHER NEARBY ANCIENT SITES

the circular walk

You are reminded that the sites described are ancient sacred places and should be respected as such. Some of the monuments lie on private farmland away from any public right of way and great care must be taken not to damage crops or frighten livestock. If in doubt always ask the farmer for permission to cross his land. Please do not leave any litter and close all field gates behind you. Thankyou.

The circular walk is described from a starting point by a medium sized lay-by adjacent to Boskenna Cross (Grid Ref.425243) on the B3315 coastal road from Penzance/Newlyn to Land's End, where there is a T-junction with a minor road to St.Buryan. Although it is possible to start a longer walk from the car park at Lamorna Cove this is usually very full during the tourist season. There are no food stores in the area but meals/refreshments are usually available from the cafe at the Cove, the village pub and Lamorna Pottery.

The 3 mile (5km) walk crosses fields and granite stiles between farms and can be very muddy in places after a rainy spell. You do have a legal right of way through any crops planted over a public footpath provided that ***you keep to the line of the path;*** *if in any doubt it is prudent to divert around field hedges.*

Boskenna Cross

In 1869 the local authority was engaged in rounding-off a ten foot thick hedge at this dangerous T-junction and it was during this work that a 2½ foot high cross-head was discovered buried within the hedge. It was then erected on a collection of stones set up to form a base and placed on a triangular piece of ground in the centre of the road junction - a position close to where it had probably stood nearly a thousand years earlier on the old churchway from Boscawen-Rose to St.Buryan.

The modern base is a peculiar mixture of assorted stones consisting of a stone roller, a millstone, and a stone with a surrounding lip and channel which may have been taken from an old cider press. The front of the cross shows a figure with large out-turned feet and wearing an above-knee length tunic. On the reverse is a cross with wide ends formed of four irregular triangular recesses with the inner part of each recess being left raised to form a low relief 'boss'. The figure of Christ is shown alive with straight limbs and erect head - a religious artform popular from about the 8th to the 12th centuries. Later on the living body was to be replaced by a corpse with arms bent, legs often crossed and head hanging to one side.

During the 1939-45 war, passing army lorries were responsible for knocking down the cross on several occasions and local representations were made to the council authorities for the monument to be moved to the side of the road to prevent further damage and this is the position where it can now be seen.

Boskenna Cross

(Langdon, 1896)

Leave the Cross by a stile tucked away in the corner of the lay-by. You are now walking a section of the ancient churchway path linking the farm of Boscawen-Rose with the parish church in St.Buryan, although many of the old field boundaries alongside which the path went have been removed - hence today the route often crosses open ground.

Follow the right-hand hedge until the final bend then cross the corner of the field to the next stile. The standing stone is straight ahead in mid-field with a wide view of the ocean beyond and the woods of St.Loy valley over to the right. Cross to the next stile.

Boscawen Ros Menhirs

Boscawen-ros Menhirs (Cooke,1989)

A fine, very gently curving menhir rises over 8 feet out of the ground of this cultivated field with a name recorded in the 1840 Tithe Apportionments as 'Long Stone'. A 7 foot high companion stone stands in the field hedge to the west but does not appear to be embedded in the ground and is therefore likely to have been torn out of its original position - a common fate for the second of a pair of stones since only one is considered necessary as a cattle rubbing post. The mid-field stone has also been recorded as having been 'knocked down' earlier this century but it is unclear whether is was re-erected on its original site. Around the turn of the century many ancient standing stones were removed from the fields in St.Buryan district as they interfered with new agricultural implements, but it was later discovered that the cattle knocked or pushed the hedges down, so that many farmers found it advantageous to "reinstate them".

The Merry Maidens would be in sight from this pair of menhirs but for the intervention of a modern hedge, and the stones are in an approximate alignment with the circle and the south-western Piper. (See 'Merry Maidens' - Michell 1.)

The way to Boscawen-Rose Farm is straightforward - locate the stile next to a gate into the farmyard then turn left; over a granite stile next to a gate and on to a minor road. Turn right, passing farm buildings, and cross a new stile into the last field on the left where the mud lane ends at field gates; then on to Tregiffian.

The next stile is of the step variety and is located between a renovated barn and small garage. The steps on the far side were deliberately broken off some years ago but the stile is now repaired and easy to cross.

FOOTPATH ALTERATIONS
CORRECTIONS TO PAGE 5 & CENTRE MAP

When you eventually arrive at a gate leading onto a rough roadway at Rosemodress, cross straight over between two houses and locate a new stile on the right-hand side beyond the buildings; another stile lies a few yards away and the route crosses two more stiles to reach a lane just to the east of Tregurnow Farm. DO NOT TAKE the farm drive northwest but follow the lane northeast that leads to the road near Lamorna Hotel. Follow the road downhill and locate a stony lane on the left hand side that goes uphill, past Menwidden and Borah Chapel, to the B3315.

Tregurnow Cross
(Langdon 1896)

TREGURNOW CROSS can be visited by taking the footpath from the old Tregurnow Pottery across a large field and then returning to the B3315. There are fine views from the cross towards St.Buryan Churchtower, the hills of Chapel Carn Brea and Bartinney, the rocky outcrop of Carn Galva, the solitary engine house of Ding Dong Mine and Roger's Tower on top of the Iron Age Hillfort of Castle-an-Dinas.

Continue walk from top of page 6.

[Turn to page 9 for continuation of the MAIN WALK]

DETOUR TO THE PIPERS STANDING STONES AND/OR BOLEIGH FOGOU. *The two huge stones of the Pipers can be seen from the 'B3315 stile' standing in fields on the far side of the road. Unfortunately there is no public right of way to this monument so you should use your common sense concerning access - there are several handy field gates. The land is part of Boleigh Farm just down the road where there is also a seasonal camp site.*

the pipers menhirs

These two massive granite standing stones are the largest menhirs to survive in Cornwall today. They are positioned about 100 yards apart in an approximate north-east to south-west alignment and are 15 and 13½ feet high respectively. Both stones were excavated around their 'feet' in 1871 but no finds were made although it was noted that the northern stone had been embedded five feet in the ground.

Ancient tradition tells of how there had once been a great battle nearby - the dead soldiers being buried beneath Boleit farmyard - and that the two stones represent the positions of the chieftains in front of their armies. The names of these chieftains were Howel and Aethelstan. This refers to the victory of the Saxon King Aethelstan over the Cornish King Howel in AD931 but there seems little doubt that the two menhirs are of the same age as the nearby Merry Maidens stone circle with whom they have such close physical and legendary links.

William Bottrell, the Victorian collector of local folklore, described how the two pipers had taken to their heels as soon as they had seen the maidens being turned into stone (for full account of the legend see under the section on the 'Merry Maidens') but that this ungallant action had failed to save them from the power of the "cursing saint, who stopped their sweet pipings, overtook them when they ran thus far, and laid them up in stone as we now see them".

In May Day festivities and revelries common in the area up until the middle of the last century it was the custom to play whistles or 'peeper' pipes made from the wood of the maythorn, however Bottrell noted that the legend of the Pipers was fairly recent and not native to West Cornwall but had been imported by visitors and then repeated by locals. He wrote how the pair of stones had always been known as the 'hurlers' from their long-standing use as a goal for the hurling run which began by the cross outside St.Buryan Church, and he went on to angrily denounce the practice of grafting modernised legends onto ancient sites as being "another example of the way in which the meaning is lost to many an ancient Cornish name (which tells a story), from the foolish desire to assimilate the expressive old Cornish name to some unmeaning English nickname". Nevertheless in spite of Bottrell's indignation stories of human beings being turned into stone occur at many ancient sites in Britain and throughout Europe and this is discussed under the 'Merry Maidens' section.

The Pipers (Blight,1861)

Alignments (after J.Michell "Old Stones of Land's End")

1. Barrow formerly at 43262469 where a Bronze Age urn was discovered during the mid-18th century = N.E.Piper = a 6 foot high standing stone near Castallack Round at 44742537 = site of an ancient chapel at Mousehole.
2. N.E.Piper = a pair of standing stones 7 and 9 feet high in a field at Higher Drift 43722830 which themselves stand on 3 alignments = a 10 foot high finely shaped standing stone on uncleared ground near Carfury 44003400 which was excavated in 1958 but without any finds being made. This stone is on 6 known alignments.
3. Tregeseal Stone Circle on the moors above St.Just = a 10 foot high standing stone at Trelew 42172693 which is on 4 known alignments. This was excavated in 1871 when human remains were found about 3 feet below the ground surface just to the north of the menhir. It was thought that these remains had been placed in the pit which had been dug to receive the stone itself = N.E.Piper.
4. See 'Merry Maidens'- Michell 1.

There are no obvious sight lines from the Pipers to existing features on the horizon but they do line up with two stones (12 & 13) on the north-west side of the Merry Maidens which are just out of sight and it is only possible to conclude that the pair of celebrated menhirs form some integral part of the stone circle "the object of which is unknown".

__BOLEIGH FOGOU__ To visit this Fogou, one of the best three such remaining monuments of its type in the County, continue walking down the B3315 road until you see a narrow stoney driveway leading left to Rosemerryn (C.A.E.R.). The Fogou lies in private grounds of this house from where permission to visit ***must be obtained.***

Boleigh Fogou

Boleigh Fogou (Cooke,1985)

A Fogou (fogo, vau etc - Cornish for 'cave') at Boleigh was first recorded in the early 18th century in an account of how a local group of Royalists had been hidden there to escape the wrath of Cromwell's supporters during the Civil War. This report mentioned a "trebble Entrenchment, in which is a Hole leading to a mighty Vault under Ground". Today no signs of this earthwork remain but the surviving stone-built fogou is among the best three in Cornwall.

The present entrance is through the broken south-west end of the long passage which curves very slightly to terminate at the collapsed northern end, the whole being roofed over with great slabs of granite which span the stone walls. An unusual L-shaped 'creep' passage leads off from the left side of the passage and rises steeply up towards ground level where it was blocked by a large stone at some unknown date. In common with other fogous (Carn Euny, Halliggye and Treveneague) this creep was likely to have been the only intended way of entering and leaving the enclosed long passage - passage ends were commonly broken out (probably during the Middle Ages) to make convenient animal shelters, domestic storehouses or hiding places for smuggled contraband. Excavation in the late 1940's discovered Iron Age pottery sherds in earth covering the floor and also a very indistinct and unfinished carving on the western upright stone by the modern entrance.

Stories common to most fogous recall how locals believed them to run for many miles under land and sea but that they were extremely dangerous places to enter on account of malevolent spirits guarding treasures hidden within. The tale of 'Duffy and the Devil' tells of how the squire, out hunting one night for hares, chased one from the Merry Maidens, past the Pipers, and down into the "Fugoe Hole". Deep inside this cave he was witness to a strange ceremony of witches - he called out to the participating Devil but was immediately obliged to run for his life with the antagonised women in close pursuit.

Fogous were constructed during the Iron Age after about 400BC until the Roman/early Christian period (3rd-4thc AD) and only occur west of the River Fal - nowhere else in Cornwall or indeed in England. They represent the continuation of indiginous 'Megalithic' traditions of stone-built passages covered by a mound. Fogou long passages invariably 'point' towards the rising or setting midsummer sun and were the most important structure of the community. No human remains have ever been found within them and their functions would seem to relate to pagan religious ceremonies and practices just prior to the introduction of Christianity.

Data (measurements approximate)
Passage Entrance 4½ft high x 5ft wide
Creep Doorway 2¾ft high x 1¼ft wide
Main Passage 36ft long x 6½ft high x 4-5ft wide
Creep 21ft long x varying height and width

After visiting the fogou and standing stones retrace your steps to the 'B3315 stile'.

CONTINUATION OF MAIN WALK *From the 'B3315 stile', cross towards a solitary telephone pole to the hedge on the far side, where there is a huge stone set in a bend (this is the stone referred to in the Merry Maidens Alignments - Barnatt 1). Cross one more stile and you are in the company of the Merry Maidens with the standing stone of Gun Rith way beyond in a field hedge.*

merry maidens stone circle

The Merry Maidens (Rev.Cotton,1826)

The Merry Maidens is a precise circle of 19 evenly spaced erect granite stones and is the best preserved monument of its type in the County. It stands slightly below the ridge of a sloping field in which cattle often graze and from which there are extensive views towards the north-west in the direction of St.Buryan churchtower and the twin hills of Bartinney and Chapel Carn Brea.

The stumpy lumps of granite making up the ring were well chosen or shaped to achieve a symmetrical effect and were set into the earth with a subtle grading so that the tallest stones are to the south-west and the shorter to the north-east - probably a mimicking of the waxing and waning phases of the moon, the sun, and indeed of life itself. The Maidens date from the Late Stone Age to Mid-Bronze Age period (approx.2500-1500BC) and in common with other stone circles in the Land's End peninsula was once surrounded by an assortment of holed stones, standing stones and barrows. The first known reference to the circle was made by William Hals (1685-1736) although he seems to have muddled it up with the stone circle at Boscawen-un to the north of St.Buryan. In 1754, Dr.William Borlase, the celebrated antiquarian vicar of West Penwith, recorded that there were 19 stones, although his original notes specified that "only two" out of the 18 stones were then "thrown down". Seventy five years later the Rev.Cotton drew the circle showing 16 stones still standing and 2 fallen (nos.2 & 3 on plan) "lying on the ground in their proper places, completely covered with heath and furze, and a third is wanting altogether" (i.e.No.16).

On Thursday 28th August 1862 an excursion was made to the antiquities of the peninsula by members of the Cambrian Archaeological

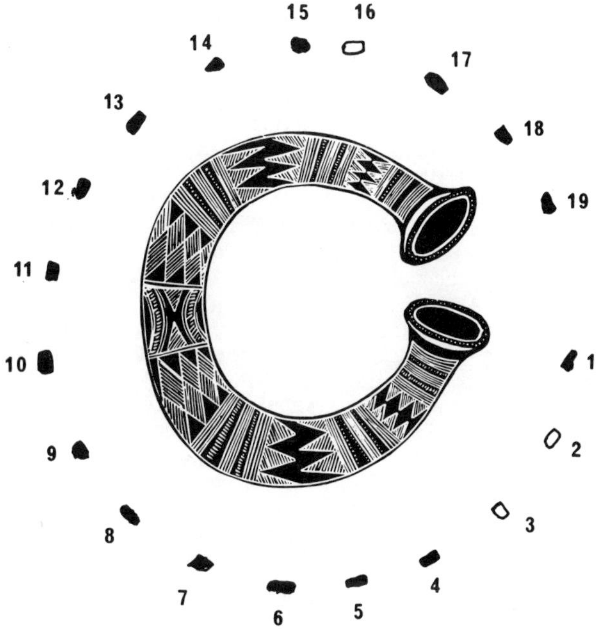

Plan of the Merry Maidens (after Barnatt,1982) and Bronze Age Torc (Cooke,1987)

Association and the subsequent report of the visit stated that "the carriages proceeded on their journey to the circle called Nine Maidens (the present Merry Maidens-Ed.), more remarkable for its perfect uninjured state than for the size of the stones forming it. The number of stones in this, also, is nineteen, in spite of its popular name..." This seems to indicate that the missing stones had been replaced by this date and although stone 2 was reset correctly, stone 3 had been placed at right angles to its proper position and stone 16 was poorly spaced, smaller than all the rest and unlikely to be one of the original stones making up the circle. A very detailed plan of 1879 shows 19 erect stones with measurements of each one and a remark in the accompanying notes that the owner of the land, Lord Falmouth, had restored one of the stones. Since then the Maidens have been allowed to remain relatively undisturbed.

18th and 19th century descriptions of the monuments surrounding the Merry Maidens infer that a second stone circle once existed in rough ground (now a field) immediately to the south-west of the present circle. All remains of this site, which may have been no more than the widely spaced kerb stones of a former barrow, were destroyed by the beginning of this century during field clearance, and it was to prevent such a fate overtaking the 'Maidens' that the then Lord Falmouth had forbidden his tenants to plough the field in which the circle stood. Vague descriptions also hint that yet a third possible circle may have stood not far away near Borah at 43752455 close to the present Churchway path from Tregurnow.

THE NAME

Pre-20th century descriptions of stone circles in Cornwall referred to them as 'Dans Men' or 'Dawns Meyn' and this has usually been interpreted as relating to their use for rituals involving dancing, or more recently to numerous stories of how standing stones may vibrate or seem to alter their position at certain times of the year. However, 'Dans Meyn' may be a straightforward mispronunciation of the Cornish phrase 'Zans Meyn' meaning 'sacred stones'. Before the industrialisation of agriculture most villages had their own sacred stone, usually a massive flat slab of granite which was highly regarded by the community but which would later be vulgarised as 'Table Maen' or 'King Arthur's Table', etc.

Although learned Victorian antiquarians might write of the 'Dans Maen', popular names for all local stone circles were the 'Merry Maidens', 'Nine Maidens', and occasionally the 'Nine Merry Maidens'. The word 'maiden' is often considered to be a simple corruption of the Cornish word for stone (men, maen, meyn - pronounced 'main') and this might well be so, but I think it also has a more literal meaning which refers to the principal type of person who used these circles for their ceremonies - groups of free unmarried women (maidens) - priestesses.

The word 'merry' is a corruption of 'Mary' which was itself derived from the name of a Middle Eastern goddess widely worshipped a thousand years before Christ. She was MA-RI, a name signifying a fruitful or fertile mother. The number 'Nine' is frequently misinterpreted in this context as being an abbreviation of nineteen - the number of stones in several of the Land's End circles. It has however nothing to do with the quantity of megaliths and often crops up in relation to ancient sites, partially remembered pagan rituals and myths. For example you must crawl nine times through the Men-an-Tol holed stone to achieve any benefits and naked children were passed clockwise nine times around Madron Well in old healing rituals. In Zennor parish anyone wishing to insure themselves against "ill-

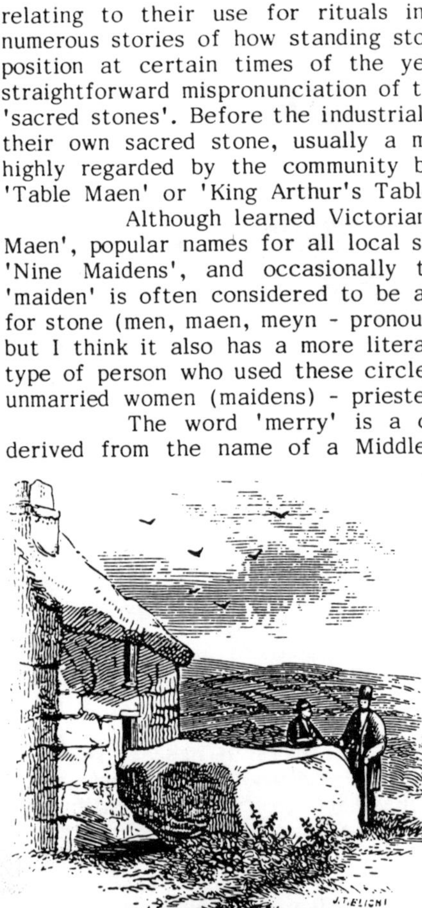

Table Men, Sennen (Blight,1861)

luck" should touch the Witches' Rock nine times at midnight and at Escalls hamlet near Sennen the local Holy Rock used to be the venue for regular evening dancing and "many old folk passed around it nine times daily, in the belief that this brought luck, besides being a protection against witchcraft".

The esoteric nature of Nine derives from the three phases of the moon and symbolises complete indestructible unending 'wholeness'. An appropriate number for a sacred location. (A full explanation of the magic of Three, Five and Nine is given in my book 'Journey to the Stones'.)

THE 'GAP'

It will quickly be observed by the visitor that the circle is apparently missing one stone on the eastern side of the ring where there is a gap almost twice as wide as that between the other stones. The circle at Boscawen-un has the same feature but on the western side, as does the much altered Tregeseal circle near St.Just. It is interesting to note that almost all of the large open stone circles of the British Isles have such a 'missing stone'.

The only way to determine whether such gaps were intentional or not is to excavate for evidence of a stone-hole but unfortunately the field in which the Merry Maidens stand was under cultivation during the last century and subjected to frequent ploughing so that any evidence within about a foot of the surface would most likely have been obliterated. There are however indications from a quite different source that such gaps were very definitely intended as an essential feature of many stone circles.

During the Bronze Age it was customary for a horseshoe-shaped ornament to be worn around the neck. These 'torcs' were often decorated with incised linear designs similar to those to be found on contemporary pottery and were made from a variety of metals from gold through to bronze. Torcs were a robust adaptation of the Early Bronze Age (c.2200BC) crescent-moon-shaped 'lunulae' - delicate thin sheets of decorated gold presumably only worn on ceremonial occasions due to their fragility. They were a personalised symbol of the moon which represented the feminine divinity considered responsible for the creation of all life. Figurines and sculptures of later Iron Age gods and lesser goddesses often show them wearing a torc, demonstrating that even they were ultimately subordinate to the Goddess.

The neck, and the torc around it, binds the body to the head and in Iron Age times Roman writers recounted how the head was considered to be the place in which the human soul resided. Yet the ends of the encircling metallic ornament did not quite meet since this would have completed a 'circle of immortality' and transported the living wearer to the 'Otherworld' through an act of strangulation, a method of sacrificial death often used in northern European pagan rituals.

While the metal torc might join body and soul for a human or even a god, so did the Dawns Meyn create a stone torc which may have had the same intended function of binding together the Earth on which the people depended for their physical existence to energies from the heavens without which the Earth could not continue to flourish. Such a torc would only be closed at periods of ritual death by completion of the ring in some way, and Richard Edmonds writing in the mid-19th century may not have been far off the mark when he wrote of the gap at the Merry Maidens that "this widest intervening space may have been for the entrance and exit of religious processions, or for bringing in and carrying out the victim".

THE LEGENDS

The Merry Maidens have become renowned through the now famous legend which tells of young girls being turned into stone for neglecting their Christian prayers. Robert Hunt, who collected much local folklore during the last century, wrote down the story as follows:-

> "In the Parish of Burian are the Dawns Myin or Men - the dancing stones - commonly called the Merry Maidens; and near them are two granite pillars, named the Pipers. One sabbath evening some of the thoughtless maidens of the neighbouring village, instead of attending vespers, strayed into the fields, and two evil spirits, assuming the guise of pipers, began to play some dance tunes. The young people yeilded to the temptation; and forgetting the holy day, commenced dancing. The excitement increased with the exercise, and soon the music and the dance became extremely wild; when lo! a flash of lightning from the clear sky transfixed them all, the tempters and the tempted, and there in stone they stand."

Other popular Victorian beliefs told how a man was buried beneath each of the stones which had been placed in their immovable positions by some "supernatural agency", and that more revellers who were said to have suffered an identical fate to the Maidens were transformed into the stones of Boscawen-un circle to the north of St.Buryan.

Such stories of irreverent humans being turned into megaliths are not confined to Cornwall. There is a remarkably similar tale attached to a former stone circle at Wulfbruchen near Neumark in Germany which was called 'Adam's Dance' or 'Stone Dance', consisting of 14 stones erected in pairs with 2 taller outlying menhirs. The legend told how there had been a dance by naked men at the site during Easter and that they had been turned into the stones as a punishment, an identical fate overtaking the two musicians outside the circle. Another example tells of how the rows of stone alignments at Carnac in Brittany had once been columns of Roman soldiers before they were miraculously petrified by the local patron saint! While nearer home there are similar stories attaching to the Nine Maidens Stone Row near St.Columb Major, the Hurlers Stone Circles on Bodmin Moor and other sites in Devon and Avon. The use of stones to commemorate tribal leaders and kings during the late Iron Age/Dark Age period and their connection with personified divinities in even earlier times, strengthened beliefs that the stones were themselves the petrified remains of human beings.

Tales of wild uninhibited dancers and musicians found expression in a number of medieval illustrations which although containing many stereotyped images of 'witchcraft', do I believe have more than a grain of truth in them. A 17th century woodcut entitled 'The Mad Merry Prank of Robin Goodfellow' depicts Goodfellow (better known as Puck the spirit of the woods and of growing vegetation) surrounded by a circle of alternate male and female dancers with a solitary musician playing some kind of horn over to one side. Puck was virtually identical with the 'Green Man',

St Buryan Churchtown

Churchyard Crosshead

Boskenna Cross

The Pipers Standing Stones

"The Mad Merry Prank of Robin Goodfellow"
(17th century ballad illustration)

traditional midsummer male sacrifice, and was later to be closely linked with the elusive legendary outlaw Robin Hood. Together with Maid Marian as his Queen, Robin appeared in the guise of the May King in the Morris dancing and dramas of the May Day (Beltane) fertility festivals celebrating the triumphal re-establishment of 'green nature' after the long months of a northern European winter.

Partially remembered events having their origins in ancient pre-Christian religious rituals have been handed down and distorted over many generations, so that human sacrifice, real or merely symbolic, of ithyphallic male companions to the priestesses have been transformed into 'men under the stones', while the dancing maidens celebrating the renewal of the earth's abundance have been turned into the stones themselves. Such deep-rooted ideas would have provided a useful half-truth to be used by the post-Reformation clergy in their propaganda against any form of idolatry - heathen or of the Roman Church - to frighten their always potentially pagan 'flock' into regular attendance of sanctioned Christian worship in the local parish church.

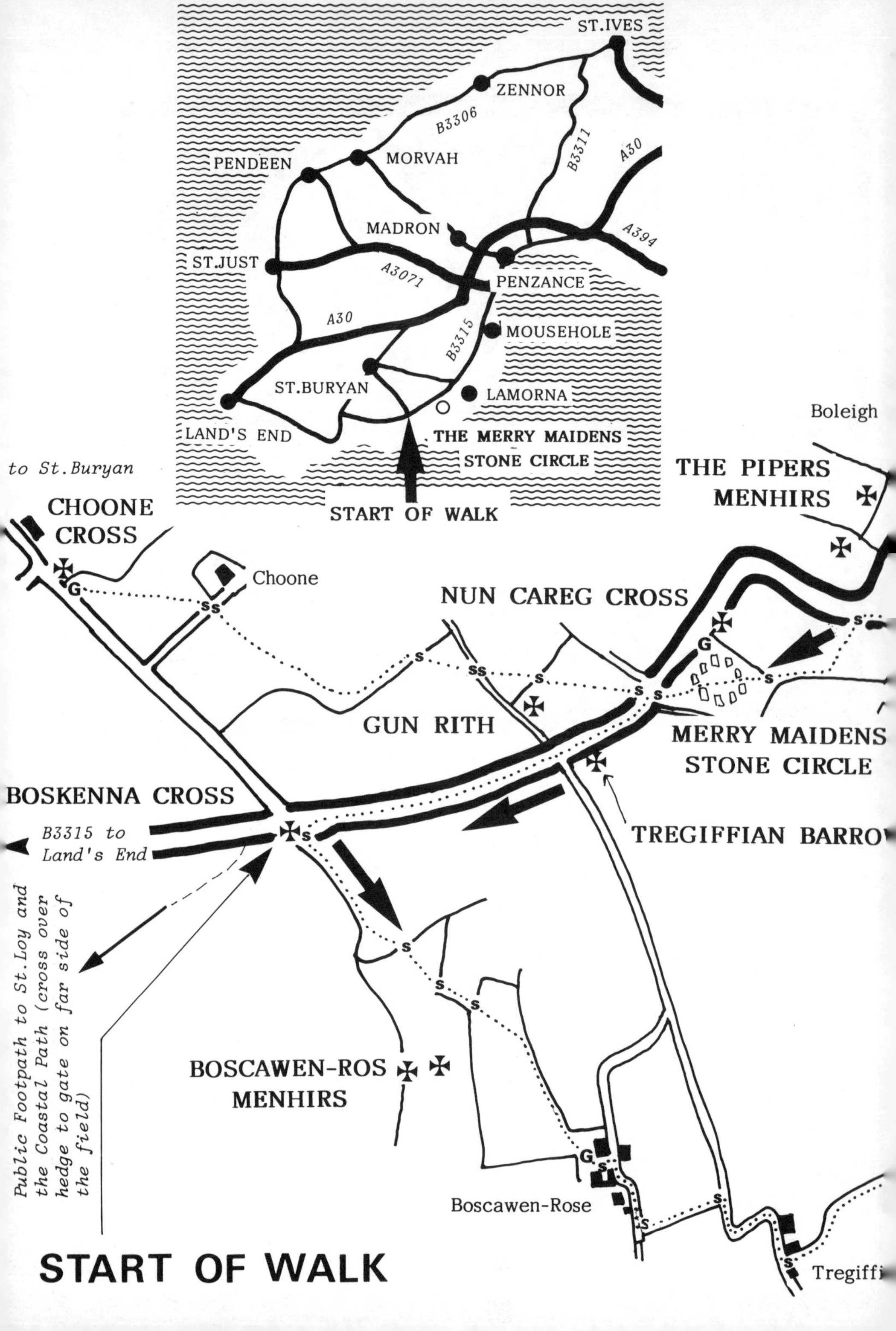

ST.IVES
ZENNOR
B3306
B3311
A30
PENDEEN
MORVAH
MADRON
A394
ST.JUST
A3071
PENZANCE
A30
B3315
MOUSEHOLE
ST.BURYAN
LAMORNA
LAND'S END
THE MERRY MAIDENS
STONE CIRCLE
START OF WALK
to St.Buryan
Boleigh
THE PIPERS
MENHIRS
CHOONE
CROSS
Choone
NUN CAREG CROSS
GUN RITH
MERRY MAIDENS
STONE CIRCLE
BOSKENNA CROSS
B3315 to
Land's End
TREGIFFIAN BARRO
Public Footpath to St.Loy and the Coastal Path (cross over hedge to gate on far side of the field)
BOSCAWEN-ROS
MENHIRS
Boscawen-Rose
START OF WALK
Tregiffi

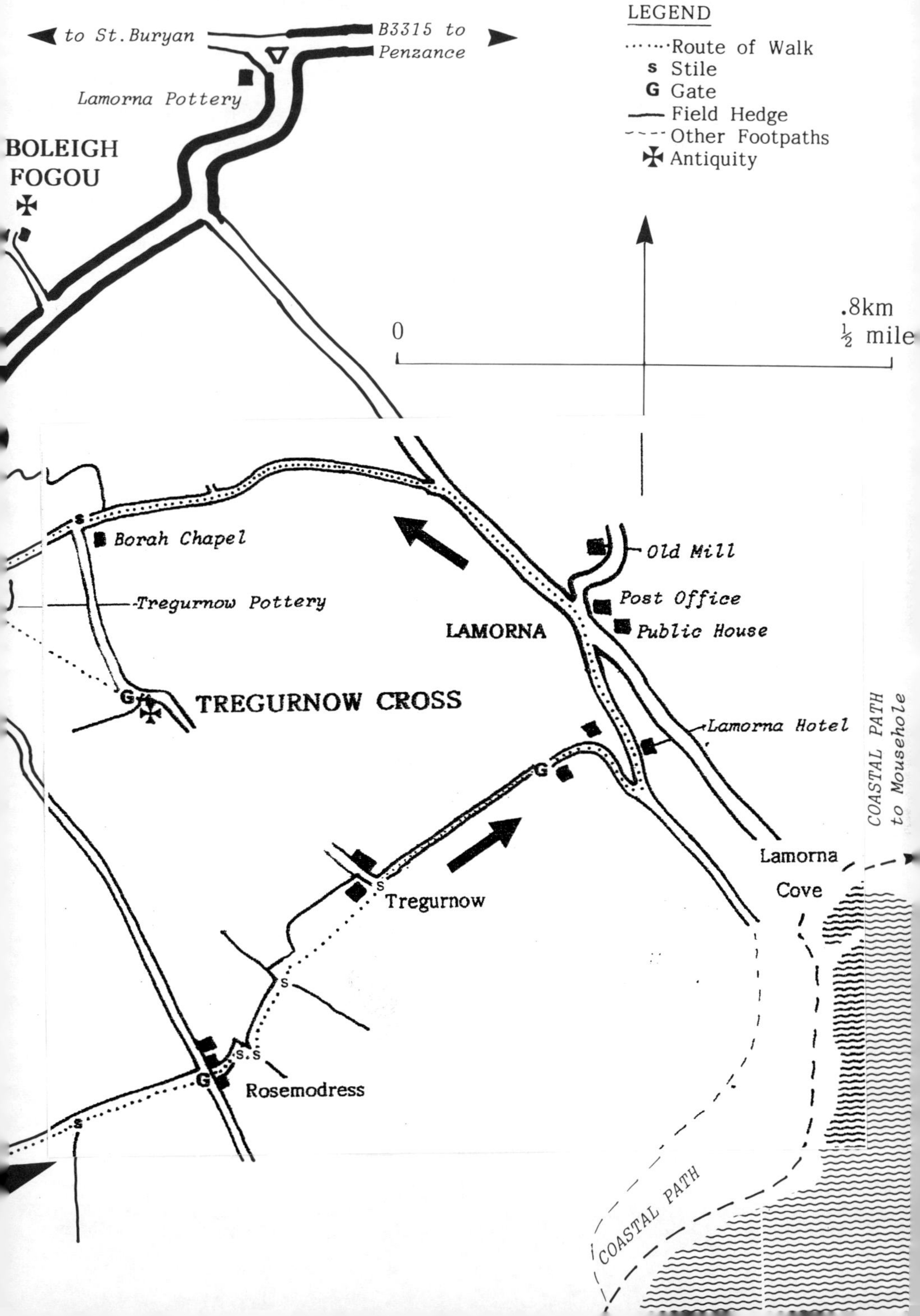
LEGEND
Route of Walk
s Stile
G Gate
Field Hedge
Other Footpaths
Antiquity
to St.Buryan
B3315 to
Penzance
Lamorna Pottery
BOLEIGH
FOGOU
0
.8km
½ mile
Borah Chapel
Tregurnow Pottery
TREGURNOW CROSS
Old Mill
Post Office
Public House
LAMORNA
Lamorna Hotel
COASTAL PATH
to Mousehole
Lamorna
Cove
Tregurnow
Rosemodress
COASTAL PATH

SOME ALIGNMENTS AT THE MERRY MAIDENS

Lockyer 1 From the circle centre to Nun Careg cross. An intervening cottage (now ruined) prevented measurement but he considered this line to refer to Arcturus, warning of the August sunrise in 1640BC. (But note that the cross is not likely to be in its original position).

Lockyer 2 & 4 and Michell 1 Lockyer considered this line to pass from the centre of the circle through a now destroyed Barrow (D) formerly in the next field and then on to the two Pipers. This was to determine the star rise position of Capella heralding the February sunrise position in 2160BC. When extended in reverse this line passes through another destroyed Barrow (B). However Michell showed how this alignment only connected with the south-west Piper and he also extended it beyond (B) to the uprooted menhir at Boscawen-Ros which now lies in a hedge.

Lockyer 3 & 5 Described as one of the chief sight lines which connected the present circle with the site of another presumed destroyed circle. This line was extended south-west to a now destroyed Barrow (L) and north-east to what Lockyer thought was the Iron Age Fogou at Boleigh but which was in fact a natural cave. He considered this alignment to have indicated the May sun rise position. There is a large recumbent stone lying amidst gorse bushes in some rough ground at Borah; this may have been a former menhir standing on or close to this alignment.

Lockyer 6 and Michell 2 This line, which marked the position of the star Antares heralding May sunrise about 1310BC, went in reverse direction through Tregiffian Barrow (A), to Boskenna Cross which Lockyer considered "doubtless a re-dressing of an old menhir". Michell extended the line on to connect with another stone cross down the road at Boskenna Gate (42012407).

Lockyer 7 and Barnatt 1 Lockyer's alignment from Gun Rith to and over the Merry Maidens marked the rising position of the Pleiades about 1960BC which would then have warned of the rising of the sun at May. Barnatt noticed that this line cut through a large stone in a hedge beyond the circle (see section on Gun Rith) and in Meyn Mamvro No.7 two other points are mentioned on this alignment - a broken stone on the ground by a 'boulder cross base' (see section on 'Nun Careg') and a possible lost third circle at 43752455 near Borah - Cornish for "place of the witch".

Lockyer 8 The bearing of St.Buryan churchtower is about N64W and Lockyer thought that the many crosses in the countryside surrounding the church had been menhirs first and crosses afterwards and that this line marked the May and August sunset position.

Meyn Mamvro 1 Boscawen-Ros (east) Menhir to the Circle centre to the north-east Piper and on to a standing stone near Sheffield at 45852752. This alignment passes close to the stump of a cut-down stone which may have been part of an adjacent Iron Age round in the field to the south-west of the Boscawen-Ros menhirs.

Note The significance of the sunrise and sunset positions in February, May, August and November is that these are the times of the four great pagan festivals of Imbolc, Beltane, Lugnasadh and Samhain. Later to be incorporated into the Christian calendar as the feasts of Candlemas, Easter/Whitsun, Lammas and All Souls/Halloween.

Sight lines from stone circles usually appear to emanate from the edge of the circle rather than from the centre.

References used

'Stonehenge and Other British Stone Monuments Astronomically Considered' by Sir Norman Lockyer (London Macmillan 1906)
'The Old Stones of Land's End' by John Michell (Garnstone Press 1974)
'Prehistoric Cornwall' by John Barnatt (Turnstone Press 1982)
'Meyn Mamvro, Ancient Stones & Sacred Sites of West Penwith' 1988/89.
'West Penwith Survey' by Vivien Russell (1971)

Beltane Maidens

Samhain Maidens

Nun Careg Cross

The Merry Maidens Stone Circle

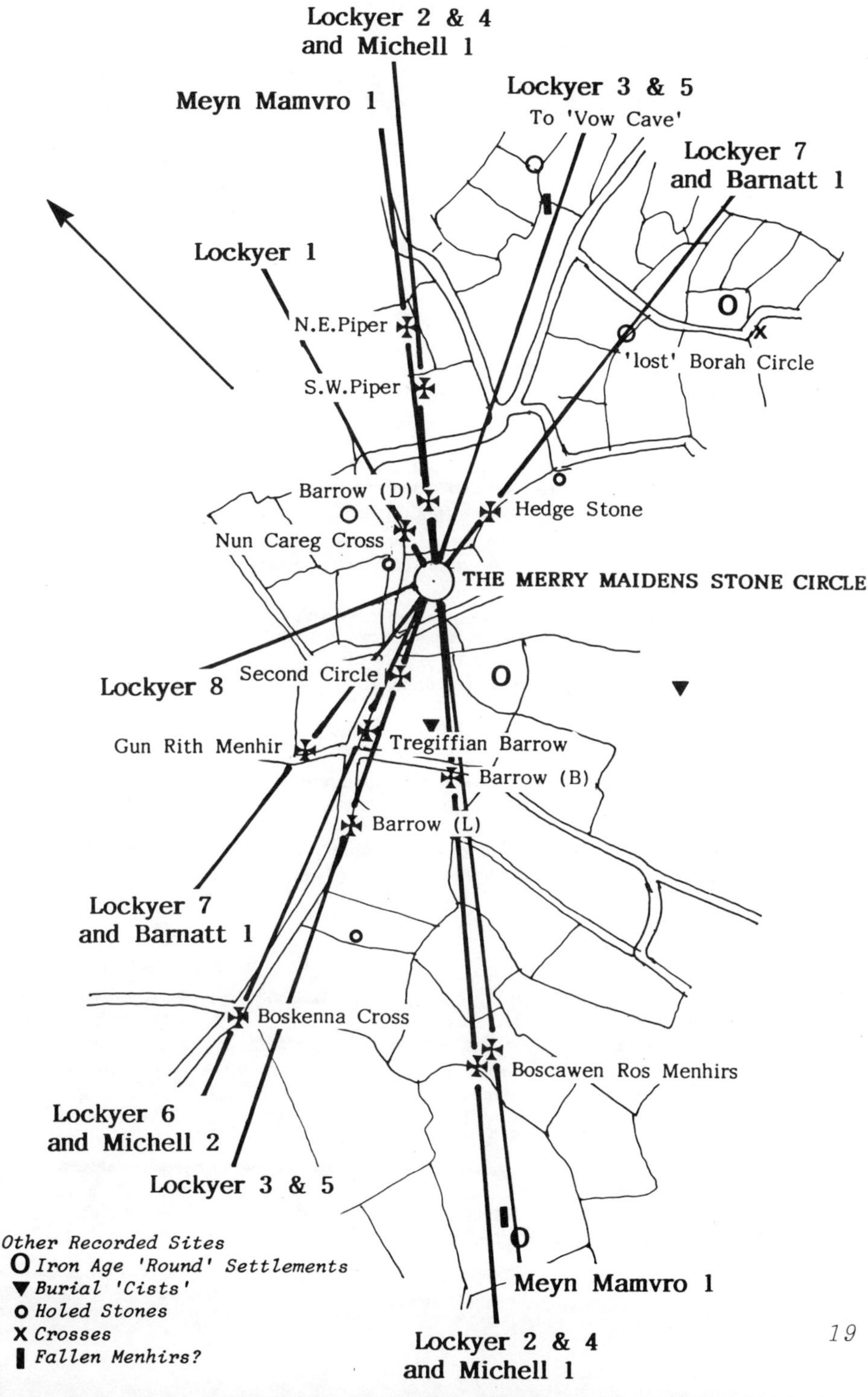
Lockyer 2 & 4
and Michell 1
Meyn Mamvro 1
Lockyer 3 & 5
To 'Vow Cave'
Lockyer 7
and Barnatt 1
Lockyer 1
N.E.Piper
S.W.Piper
'lost' Borah Circle
Barrow (D)
Hedge Stone
Nun Careg Cross
THE MERRY MAIDENS STONE CIRCLE
Lockyer 8
Second Circle
Gun Rith Menhir
Tregiffian Barrow
Barrow (B)
Barrow (L)
Lockyer 7
and Barnatt 1
Boskenna Cross
Boscawen Ros Menhirs
Lockyer 6
and Michell 2
Lockyer 3 & 5
Meyn Mamvro 1
Lockyer 2 & 4
and Michell 1
Other Recorded Sites
Iron Age 'Round' Settlements
Burial 'Cists'
Holed Stones
Crosses
Fallen Menhirs?

ALIGNMENTS, LEYS and STONE CIRCLES

The first serious attempt to discover alignments at the Merry Maidens was made by Sir Norman Lockyer who produced a complete survey of the ancient sites in the area during October 1905. Three months later he returned to test out his theory on site that the two Pipers had been placed in a direct line with the centre of the circle and as part of this project he had a section of an intervening hedge removed. The results of his studies were drawn up in table form and showed 8 sight lines to possible astronomical markers. The next detailed assessment of alignments was made by John Michell nearly 70 years later and published in his 'Old Stones of Land's End'.

However at least two of Lockyer's alignments are physically inaccurate. In his line 2/4 the Pipers do not align with the centre of the stone circle and Michell wrote how a recent survey (1970's) showed them to be aligned with two stones on the north-western segment (Nos. 12 & 13 ? on plan). This relatively minor error was compounded by one of major proportions in that Lockyer had confused the site of the Iron Age Fogou or 'vow' at Boleigh (in the grounds of Rosemerrin house at 437252) with a natural cave marked on the 6 inch O.S. map as 'Vow Cave' (at 44752520) by Castallack Carn on the far side of Lamorna valley (see his alignment 3/5). Nevertheless in spite of these inaccuracies his general approach to examining ancient sites as part of an all-embracing whole and their relationship with the sky and approaching seasons, remains essentially sound.

The building of stone circles evolved out of the existing prehistoric culture after about 3500BC and continued until approximately 1500BC. There is no evidence that stone circles were an imported ritual structure and over 900 still exist throughout the British Isles. Circles, along with the other monuments of the Megalithic (great stone) Culture were carefully sited in the landscape and many have very definite relationships with underground streams, hills and rocky outcrops, as well as with significant events taking place in the sky throughout the year. Stone circles should not be considered in isolation but as part of a comprehensive system of structures built to be of practical use throughout the seasonal cycles that repeated year after year, and whose continuation was essential to the life of the tribal communities who spent so much effort and skill in the building of their sacred sites.

CONCLUSION

That the Merry Maidens Stone Circle was used for ceremonial religious purposes cannot seriously be doubted. The **Legends** of wild abandoned dancing at dusk with vague hints of male sacrifice in fertility rituals; the **Name** having connotations of sacred stones, officiating priestesses, the magical moon number Nine, and fertile Mother Goddess; the **Alignments** announcing the approaching seasons; the deliberate **Design** of the graded stones and the **Gap** with connections to the Moon Goddess and journeys beyond death. All these indicate that this stone circle was an exceptionally sacred place dedicated to the principle of female creation - the Goddess - - tended by priestesses of the moon officiating at ceremonies intended to promote and continue the prosperity and abundance of the people, the animals, the crops and the Earth herself.

From the Stone Circle walk down the field to the main B3315 road. ***DETOUR TO NUN CAREG*** *The Cross stands in the grass verge just beyond a gate leading into the top of the 'Maidens field'. Directly opposite this gate is a holed stone used as a gatepost, but whether this is prehistoric is doubtful since the hole is straight-edged and looks as if it was drilled through.*

NUN CAREG CROSS

This handsome little cross stands by the roadside just to the north of the Merry Maidens. On the front is a 'Latin' cross with the arms widening towards the extremities and with its longer lower limb being carried down the shaft - an additional small cross has been cut into the stone at the intersection of the arms. The cross on the reverse is unusual in that it was cut partly in relief and partly by an incised line.

The stone became separated from its base at an unknown date but may once have stood in a cross-socket cut into a large natural boulder a few hundred yards downhill just off the main road in a disused lane by the stile leading into the 'Gun Rith' field. A broken flat circular stone with a square-cut hole in the centre lies by the roadside a few yards from the boulder cross base - it could have been a mill stone or alternatively a newer base made for the cross which may have been moved to be adjacent to the realigned churchway path. The field immediately next to this socket was called 'Cross Field' in the 1840 Tithe Apportionments and the line of the present footpaths from this south-eastern part of the parish towards St.Buryan was once a principal churchway passing through the Merry Maidens, past Gun Rith standing stone and on to join the minor road to St.Buryan by another ancient cross at Choone.

Many assumed Christian crosses are likely to have had their origins as pagan standing stones and an interesting quotation is given below showing the continuity of worship of such stones.

In AD658 a Council assembled at Nantes decreed that "As in remote places and in woodlands there stand certain stones which the people often worship, and at which vows are made, and to which oblations are presented - we decree that they all be cast down and concealed in such a place that their worshippers may not be able to find them. Now the carrying out of their order was left to the country parsons, and partly because they themselves had been brought up to respect these stones, and partly because the

Nun Careg Cross (Blight,1856)

execution of the decree would have brought down a storm upon their heads, they contented themselves with putting a cross op top of the stones." (from "Book of Brittany" by Baring-Gould)

CONTINUATION OF MAIN WALK *On the far side of the road from the Maidens, at the start of an old overgrown lane, are the remains of a broken millstone and a few yards behind it a cross socket cut into a great rounded boulder (referred to above). The way to the Gun Rith standing stone is now obvious from the map.*

Gun Rith Menhir

The name of this fine ten and a half foot high (3.2m) stone means the Red Downs - a name seized upon by Victorian antiquarians who longed to associate all ancient sites with scenes of blood-shed, sacrifice and long-forgotten battles. The ground around it's base was excavated by Copeland Borlase in 1871 but only a worn sandstone pebble was found, possibly a whetstone. When viewed from Gun Rith, the gap in the Merry Maidens is bisected by Stone 10 of the circle almost due east and this may have had connections with the rising sun or full moon at the equinox. A distant sight could have been provided by the large stone in the hedge to the east of the circle (see below) which would have been in view before the modern hedges were built. An observer on the rising ground to the west of Gun Rith would probably have been able to sight along the tops of Gun Rith, Stone 10 and the 'Hedge Stone'.

Gun Rith (Cooke, 1989)

Alignments

Michell found no alignments from this stone but Barnatt mentioned two "curious non-astronomical alignments" between the Merry Maidens and outlying standing stones, one of which went from Gun Rith to the centre of the circle and then on to a great flattish slab of stone about 6 feet high and 4 feet wide now forming part of the hedge beyond the circle (this is the

'Hedge Stone' mentioned above). This alignment, but without the Hedge Stone, was noticed by Lockyer who stated that it cut across many ancient stones, mostly fairly insignificant, but regarded this line as a possible "old 'via sacra' for processions between the circle and the monolith". He was unable to find any astronomical use for Gun Rith when viewed from the circle but there was an "obvious" alignment in the reverse direction which would have marked the position of the Pleiades about 1960BC -a group of stars warning of the rising May sun.

Return to the roadside stile after visiting this stone - please keep to the hedge and line of footpath.

Tregiffian Barrow

Tregiffian Barrow (Cooke, 1989)

This barrow lies right on the very edge of the road whose construction in about 1840 was largely responsible for its mutilation and it was another of the many sites excavated by Copeland Borlase during the 19th century.

Once the covering of turf had been removed it was discovered that the barrow had been previously "overhauled"; many of the stones being removed to make the roadside hedges nearby and with the missing stones then being replaced with mud and general refuse. This was probably the work of the road builders thirty years earlier. The barrow chamber had been constructed of large vertically placed slabs of granite which were then spanned by much larger and longer flat stones to make a wide 'passage' closed at the inner end. The capstone nearest to the chamber entrance had been dislodged by an eleven foot 'longstone' which Borlase thought had once stood on top of the barrow mound. Although modern excavation reports insist that it was one of the roofing lintels it's shape looks far more like a traditional standing stone - it is now one of the stones making up the restored roof. Borlase found a great quantity of ashes and splintered bone underneath the dislodged capstone and more of the same from beneath a flat stone lying on the floor of the chamber. Some cremated remains were discovered in a small pit which had been lined with shell sand peculiar to Porthcurno beach over three miles away which is not the nearest source of beach sand. No pottery or metal artifacts were unearthed at this time.

Additional important features were however revealed when the site was again investigated during the late 1960's. The floor of the chamber was still strewn with bits of bone and ashes but two additional pits which had been missed by the Victorian excavators were found under this debris, one of which contained an undamaged urn. The most fascinating find was the discovery that the eastern flanking stone to the entrance was covered with an apparently random design of 'cupmarks', thirteen circular and twelve oval. The original stone is now in the County Museum Truro and has been replaced on site by a concrete replica! Other cupmarked stones found in the barrow now seem to have been lost but a large cracked stone with a single big cupmark was found lying in the south-east part of the barrow and this has now been positioned as one of the new capstones supported underneath by an iron girder. It was deduced from these excavations that the barrow had originally only consisted of an earthen mound containing the chamber, with the whole being enclosed and retained by a ring of vertically placed 'kerb-stones' - the typical form of West Penwith 'entrance grave'. This stage was dated to between about 3000-2000BC. The stone kerb had later on been replaced by the arrangement that can be seen today.

The numbers twelve and thirteen which appear on the cupmarked entrance stone are both highly significant. In any solar year there are either 12 full moons and 13 new moons or 12 new moons and 13 full moons.

Data

The diameter of the barrow is about 50 feet (15m) with the chamber being approximately 15 feet long by 6 feet wide and from 2½-3½ feet high (4.5 x 1.8 x 1 metres). The entrance faces just west of south.

The final 10 minutes of this walk back to Boskenna Cross, which I hope you have enjoyed, is along the busy B3315 road - take care.

menhirs

'Menhir' is a Cornish word derived from 'men' or 'maen' (stone) and 'hyr' or 'heere' (long) - hence Longstone. It is used in this context to describe a standing stone put up during the prehistoric period.

Tall standing stones are found in many areas of the British Isles and in Cornwall they are heavily concentrated in the Land's End peninsula where they have a greater density than anywhere else in Britain. They are also prevalent across the Channel in Brittany - a region that in prehistory West Cornwall was closer to, both culturally and economically, than with 'up-country' Britain.

Limited excavations around the base of a number of menhirs show that they were erected during the same period that the majority of stone circles were being built (i.e. Early and Middle Bronze Age approximately 2500-1500BC) and therefore formed part of the same culture. Locally they are found singly or as a pair of standing stones in close proximity.

A basic problem both for professional archaeologists and the amateur enthusiast is how to differentiate between a genuine Bronze Age standing stone and a modern 'rubbing post' for cattle. The majority of menhirs probably owe their survival into the late 20th century to their usefulness as rubbing posts and many farmers have supplemented this meagre supply of ancient stones by erecting their own - often in the centre of a field. Ideally a rubbing stone should be about the height of a cow's back (4-5 feet or 1.2-1.5 metres) although a larger stone might be utilised if it was handy. Nevertheless, stones over about 7 or 8 feet in length (2.1-2.4m) would normally have been too much trouble to move, at least before the common agricultural use of the JCB (i.e.before about the 1950's), so that it is reasonably safe to assume that stones over this height are ancient menhirs, and conversely that stones under about 4 feet (1.2m) in fields are also ancient - Bronze Age sites often used quite small stones (see Merry Maidens).

In common with other classes of prehistoric site it is the purpose of putting up such weighty lumps of granite that is so elusive - why was so much trouble and effort expended? During the early 1870's the ground around the base of about half a dozen menhirs was examined for the purpose of establishing whether they had been "sepulchral monuments", and further excavations were carried out during this century at Carfury, Try and Kerrowe. Results, although sparse, make it clear that marking burials was not the primary function and in some cases huge stones had been transported across several miles of rough country to a predetermined destination. Suggestions as to possible function range from boundary marks, meeting places, guideposts and for fertility practices or "other more obscure rites" for which human remains had been used as offerings. This suggestion of a possible ritualistic function is further strengthened by the discovery of nine white quartzite pebbles in a pit close by a menhir formerly on Longstone Down near St.Austell, and a layer of quartz around the Men Gurta near Wadebridge. The significance of quartz and the number Nine both relate to the moon, death and continuity through rebirth. Another strong pointer towards a ritual function lies in the orientation of pairs of standing stones which is frequently in a north-east to south-west or north-west to south-east alignment relating to major turning points in the solar and lunar years. At least one menhir has been shown to have replaced a previous wooden post and an intermediate small standing stone, the sequence suggesting that there was a continuity of use of the site over many years.

Menhirs often have astronomical functions with other sites and all seem to have been placed in the ground to mark underground water courses or geological faults. They acted as a focus linking the energies of the sky to the energies of the earth, with the essentially masculine shape of the stone often being emphasised by deliberate shaping. Yet in essence these great menhirs were not simple idols to be worshipped but functioned as virile male members fertilising the earth itself.

Ancient functions of fertility lingered on into the folklore of relatively modern times and many stones were visited by women with the purpose of curing barrenness or to ensure an easy childbirth. Links with ancient rituals concerned with the sun, moon and seasons ensured that these stones were identified with the Otherworld to whom offerings would be made in an effort to appease the spirits and 'tap into' the never-ending supply of strength represented by the rigid and erect stone pillar.

commune to kingdom

There are two main watersheds in the prehistory of the British Isles which changed existing societies in a fundamental way and determined the direction that tribal life was to take for many generations.

The first occurred around the early part of the 5th millenium BC when northern Europe enjoyed a milder climate, with clearer skies and calmer seas; forests and marshes covered much of the lowland landscape and today's moorlands were then lush grasslands. New farming techniques were introduced with hithertoo unknown types of domesticated animals and cereal crops as well as polished stone tools and pottery. The more settled lifestyle of the new immigrants (Neolithic or New Stone Age period) made a considerable impact on the environment as land was cleared for agriculture.

Traditional tribal societies were always based on a number of clans united by ties of blood relationships, with individuals having well defined customary duties and obligations towards each other. Wealth tended to be communal and marriage was a loose easily dissolved arrangement within the clan group characterised by ancestral descent through the mother as the only authenticated parent.

It was only once a surplus of food could be produced above that needed for simple survival that some people were able to take part in activities not requiring manual labour in the fields. How long this took is unknown but it was a significant step forward and allowed full-time specialisation in a host of non-agricultural pursuits. One consequence of this was the flowering after about 3500BC of a fascinating and elusive culture involving the erection and use of huge stone monuments - The Megalithic Culture - resulting in thousands of quoits, chambered barrows, holed stones, circles and standing stones being carefully sited throughout the countryside.

Centuries of specialisation gave opportunities for personal enrichment and these possibilities made serious inroads into traditional tribal life with its community of

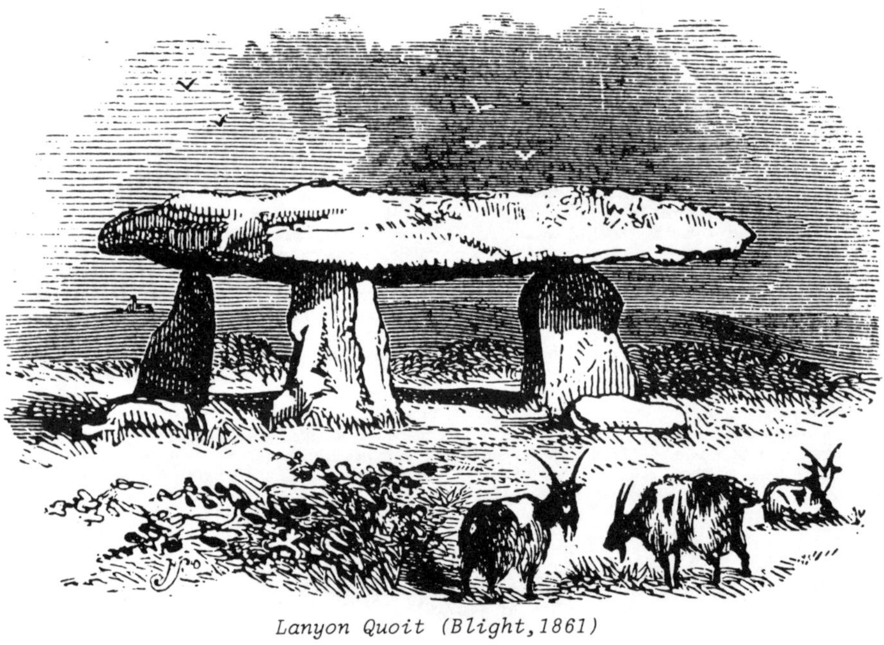

Lanyon Quoit (Blight, 1861)

equals. The advent of gold, copper and bronze work (early Bronze Age c.2500BC) took generations to effect profound alterations to society but new technologies were slowly increasing social divisions.

A second major change seems to have begun during the centuries after about 1500BC and is marked archaeologically by the running down of megalithic construction, the abandonment of many settlements with associated field systems and their substitution by a culture revolving around great hillforts.

External pressures from continental and neighbouring warrior tribes, and internal friction between long-standing 'matriarchal' cultures with the rising importance of military activities and male personal property accumulation was to lead eventually to a 'patriarchal' society in which ancestry and wealth passed directly from father to son. Such a momentous event must surely have resulted in drastic alterations in religious ritual and ceremonial structure to suit the new conditions. Population was tending to outstrip the productivity of available land, and this, allied to a relentless deterioration in the climate aggravated an already volatile situation.

Expansion could only be achieved by encroaching on neighbouring territory and the abilities of war leaders became crucial as aggressive tendencies intensified. This trend resulted in tribal warrior chieftains being 'elected' from within the most influential family clans and was to lead eventually to an hereditary royalty founded on successful leadership in war.

The arrival of Celtic iron technology into western Britain around 400BC acted as a catalyst to speed up existing Bronze Age tribal and inter-tribal tensions. The Celts were never a racial or national entity but a collection of tribes having their homelands in central Europe, an economy centred around the working of iron, and extensive trade connections with classical Greek and Oriental-inspired cultures. Their influence into south-west Britain was one of culture and was carried along the age-old maritime routes to Gaul and Iberia (modern France, Spain and Portugal) parts of which had been settled by Celtic tribes. The old unstable paired marriage, commonplace before the dominance of private wealth, was gradually being replaced by a more rigid patriarchal family comprising several generations of descendants from one man. This was to be the common form of the family in much of Europe until early Victorian times and reflected the desire of men with property and wealth to pass this on within the clan structure to their own natural sons and heirs.

As the centuries passed by, the position of these 'free farmers' became desperate. Unable to compete economically with the slave-run estates of the warrior chieftains and usually too weak militarily to repell attacks by hostile neighbouring clans, many were

The Men-an-Tol (Rev.Cotton,1826)

compelled to seek protection from a powerful 'lord' in return for giving up their land titles - so becoming tenant serfs.

Iron Age society became more class structured as differences in wealth and opportunity intensified. At the top were the warriors with riches of cattle, land and precious metals; then came the mass of 'free farmers', and finally the lowest group consisting of serfs and slaves - victims of inter-tribal warfare and internal tribal class oppression. Standing above all were the Druids, the educated class - guardians of secular and religious knowledge. The beliefs over which they officiated stretched back to the Neolithic and had grown out of a close partnership with nature and the elements - rituals and ceremonies being modified over generations to suit ever changing tribal priorities and psychological needs.

By the 5th/6th centuries AD, this 'Old Religion', already corrupted by the divisions within society, was coming under intense ideological pressure from the rising popularity of Christianity which had been brought to the British Isles by elements of the Roman settlement. Irish and Welsh armed settlers arriving in the south-west were accompanied by holy men and women, often ex-Druids, who spearheaded the conversion of local chiefs. Many of the springs, wells and other sacred pagan locations were dedicated to Saints and early Celtic Christianity, rooted firmly in the rural traditions of paganism, but preaching the universal brotherhood of man (within limits), was to play a vital role in the transformation of society with the creation of kingdoms over-riding ancient fragmented tribal boundaries.

Choone Cross (Blight,1856)

SUGGESTED FURTHER READING

"THE SECRET COUNTRY" by J & C Bord (Paladin Granada 1978) also "EARTH RITES" (Paladin Granada 1982)
"THE OLD STONES OF LAND'S END" by J.Michell (Pentacle Books 1979)
"A GUIDE TO THE MEGALITHS OF EUROPE" by Bradbury & Service (Paladin Granada 1981)
"MEYN MAMVRO - Ancient Stones & Sacred Sites of West Penwith" quarterly magazine available from local bookshops or direct from the Editress, 51 Carn Bosavern, St.Just, Penzance. TR19 7QX.

how to get there without a car

The two places closest to the Merry Maidens which are served by public transport are Mousehole and St.Buryan. The former has a frequent bus service to and from Penzance until late in the evening, whereas the service to St.Buryan is limited to only a few buses dispersed throughout the day. It is suggested therefore that you take a morning bus from Penzance to Land's End and alight at the village of St.Buryan (about a 25 minute journey) where there are several shops and a public house.

From ST.BURYAN

It is just over a one hour walk to the Merry Maidens. From the village walk down 'Rectory Road' next to the Post Office for about 1½ miles (2½km.) - there is a short cut across one field via a granite stile - until just past a turning on the right to Downs Barn Farm; note an ancient stone cross (Choone Cross) on the left side of the road. Now keep a look out for a wooden field gate on the left, by the side of which is a ruinous stone stile. From this spot you can see the stone circle in a field about ¾ mile away and the public right of way goes towards it in an almost straight line. This is the most interesting way to approach the circle and was originally part of an old churchway from the south-eastern part of the parish. Choone Cross marked the junction with another churchway from Boscawen-Rose Farm.

Cross into the large field and walk in the direction of a house roof (Choone) and over two stiles spanning a new private road. Walk uphill, towards and across some uncleared ground, until you reach a field hedge. Follow this along to the left (ignoring any turns or gaps) until you eventually find a stone stile someway down the slope of a hill. Cross into a cultivated field and walk in a line aiming slightly to the right of the Maidens, then via two half-concealed stiles spanning an old overgrown lane and into another field. Gun Rith Standing Stone is just along the line of the hedge to the right. Now follow the directions for the main walk (page 21).

For the direct route to Mousehole from the Merry Maidens follow the minor road and lane past Borah Chapel to the old Lamorna Post Office (see map in centre pages) and continue by the well-marked and scenic coastal path from Lamorna Cove, or across country through the Kemyel Farms along public footpaths (see map opposite). The total walk from St.Buryan to Mousehole, allowing plenty of time for sightseeing along the way, should take about 4-5 hours and is approximately 7 miles (12km) in length.

From MOUSEHOLE

It is about a 4 mile (7km) walk (2 hours) from Mousehole Harbour to the Merry Maidens Stone Circle. The walk is over reasonably level ground except for a steep climb out of Mousehole and the drop into Lamorna Valley.

From the Bus Terminus by the war memorial on the harbour front, walk on past the Ship Inn and the Lobster Pot Restaurant to follow the road around to the right; where it bends sharply to the left by Pam's Pantry CARRY STRAIGHT ON up a narrow alleyway 'Cherrygarden Street'. After the steps at the end, turn sharp left along the path, past 'Treen Villas', after which the tarmac changes to a mud path going steeply uphill to eventually cross a driveway. Immediately opposite is a flight of granite steps leading up to the first of many fields. Walk uphill aiming to the left of a telephone pole to locate the first stile. From now on the route should be clear to Raginnis hamlet with its 18th century thatched cottage. Further on there is a very small Latin cross- head in a field hedge to the right of the path - also many standing stones, probably mostly of modern origin for use as cattle rubbing posts. On to Kemyel Drea where the route goes between farm buildings via a gate and several wooden stiles, continue along a 'green lane' and over a granite slab footbridge spanning some boggy ground amidst a small wood of huge hawthorn and sloe bushes.

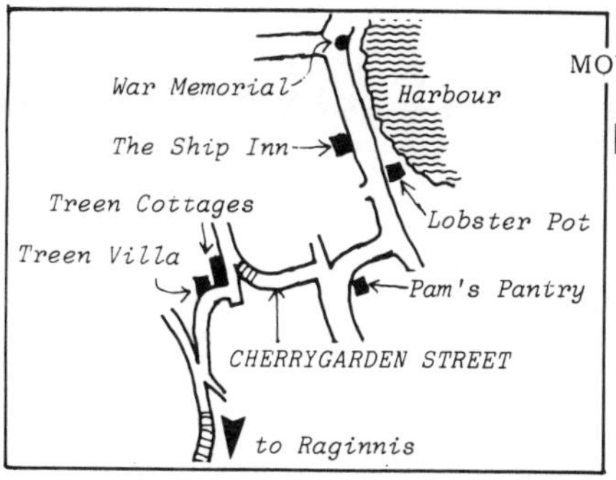

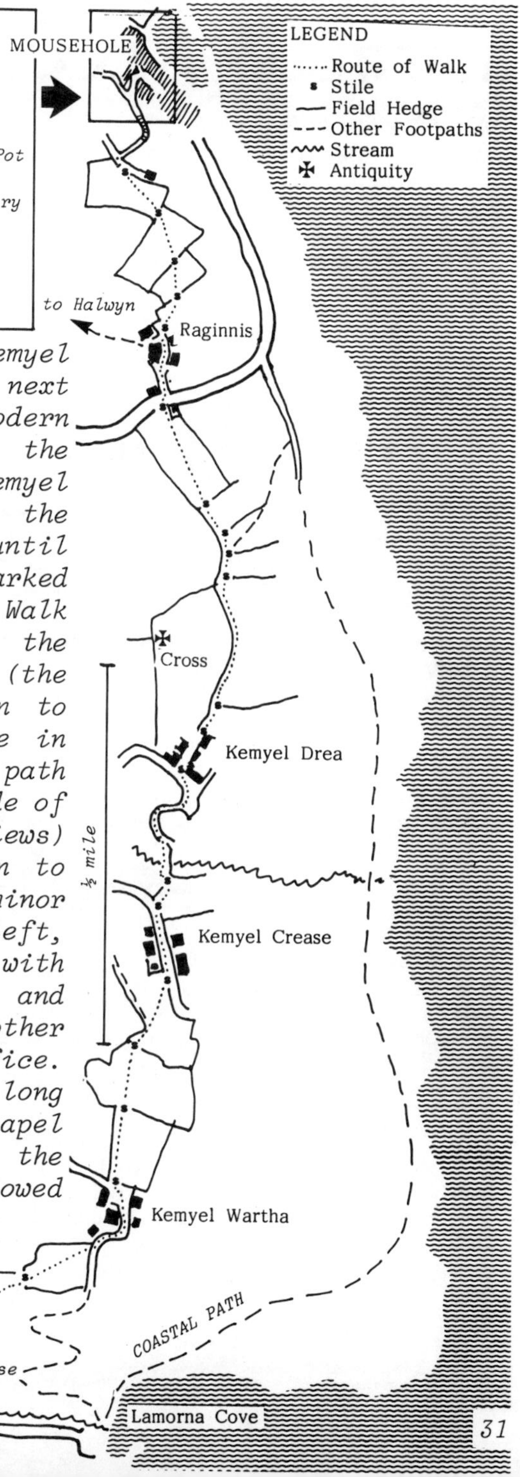

Follow the road through Kemyel Crease to locate the next stile just past a modern bungalow, then keep to the line of stiles to Kemyel Wartha, again following the roadway through the farm until you arrive at a waymarked junction of paths. Walk through the wide gap on the right and into the field (the left hand path goes down to Lamorna Cove) to a stile in the far lower corner. The path now meanders along the side of the valley (wonderful views) to eventually plunge down to exit at a stile by the minor road to Castallack. Turn left, passing the Old Mill Shop with its attendant peacocks and ducks, and on to meet another road by the old Post Office. Turn right and locate the long rough lane to Borah Chapel where directions for the Circular Walk can be followed (see page 6).

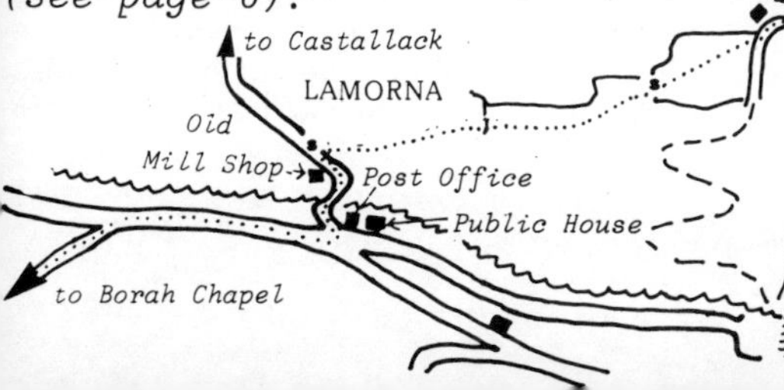

journey to the stones

WALKS, STONES AND CELTIC MYSTERIES - Eight comprehensively described walks with detailed maps take you to over 40 prehistoric and early Christian sites, including all the 'quoits' and stone circles in the Land's End peninsula, as well as a selection of holy wells, inscribed stones, standing stones, barrows, hillforts, crosses and settlements. The esoteric associations of certain trees, plants and flowers; mermaids; phallic moonstones; the Celtic Sun God Bran; midsummer and midwinter sacrifices; pagan festivals and the magic of metals; all are woven into the walks and linked to the ancient stones. Other sections investigate the symbolisms of sun, moon, and certain numbers - why are there always nine maidens, never eight or ten? And how does the new crescent moon give life to the dying sun?

mother and sun

This monumental work is the first comprehensive assembly of material on Iron Age Cornish souterrains (fogous) ever to have been printed. The co-operation of individuals and institutions has enabled many hitherto unpublished drawings, diagrams, photographs and plans to be used. The book contains a wealth of information relating to the orientation of fogou passages towards the sun and their relationship with underground mineral lodes, folklore, the prehistoric tin trade, and a collection of 'fogomania'. The idea that fogous were originally sacred places associated with rituals of the pre-Roman religion of West Cornwall has, until now, been largely based on purely subjective opinion; but Ian Cooke's holistic approach to his subject enables convincing links to be made between the architecture and alignment of fogou passages, archaeological discovery, ancient mythology and contemporary art-forms, which lead in conclusion to some fascinating and startling conclusions.

JOURNEY TO THE STONES by Ian Cooke [ISBN 0-9512371-0-1] £8.95.
160 pages 244 x 184mm sewn in sections; can be opened out without falling to pieces as often happens with glued pages. Many black and white illustrations and photographs. Signed copies available direct from the author at the Men-an-Tol Studio (please add £1.50 for postage).

MOTHER AND SUN - THE CORNISH FOGOU by Ian Cooke
[ISBN 0-9512371-6-0] £38. This work, which will not be reprinted or later published in paperback, is printed in a limited edition of only 1000 copies, each numbered and signed by the author. Hardback, 352 pages, 244 x 184mm, with full colour dust jacket, and comprehensively illustrated with over 120 line drawings, plans and maps, and over 90 photographs depicting not only the actual monuments but also the magnificent countryside within which the fogous are located. Copies available direct from the author at Men-an-Tol Studio (post free).